GOOD MANNER ALPHABETS

How to be a super polite kid!

Texts & Illustrations
by

OPHELIA S. LEWIS

Available in Paperback, PDF Flipbook, eBook and 24" x 36" Jumbo Poster
ISBN: 978-0-985-36251-5
LCCN 2012953224
eISBN: 978-0-985-36255-3

Cover design by OASS

Published by Village Tales Publishing
Printed in the U.S.A.

DEDICATED TO

Team-Sapo Seniors

ANTHONY Nah * BRANDON Penn

CAMYRN Dawson * CHRISTIAN Dawson

DANIEL Mooney * FAITH Nah

HAWA John-Lewis * KAELA White

KAI Dawson * MARY Mooney

MYLAEKA Lewis

AND Team-Sapo Juniors

CARTER John-Lewis * COBI Dawson

ELIJAH Lewis * ETHAN Cason

HALLE John-Lewis * KAYDEN Dawson

LILLIAN Hayde * LOGAN Matthews

LONDON Matthews * LYDIA Matthews

MARLEY Dendy * NORA Hayde

RHEA Bolton * RYAN Bolton

Join Team-Sapo, we want more members
Email: kid_sapo@yahoo.com

Give feedback on this book at author's website www.ophelialewis.com
or email ophie2020@yahoo.com

Hello, I'm Sapo!

Did you know that *courteous* boys and girls **ALWAYS** practice polite habits when they're at home, *at play*, at school, and while SITTING at the table too? Consideration for others is a *good way* to start. You must learn GOOD manners to be thoughtful, kind and smart. Are You A Super Polite Kid? No WORRIES. To be a *Super Polite Kid*, it's as easy as the ABCs. *Learn*, and then REMEMBER, to follow these SIMPLE RULES...

Sapo

Earn a certificate too
after you've learned your
GOOD MANNER ALPHABETS!

A B C D E F
G H I J K L
M N O P Q R S
T U V W X Y Z

Don't be tardy,
Arrive On Time
When the recess bell chime,
Join your friends and
Romp! Romp! Romp!

If gloomy or moody,
Or in a hasty pace;
When Mommy says,
"BE PATiENT."
Settle down, stay calm,
And wait for Mom.

Open doors. Close doors.
Go out. Come in.
Hold doors open for others,
And remember to
CLOSE DOORS QUIETLY

When you're not very nice,
Or really, really mad,
And mainly when put in timeout;

Don't Pout

You are of age to sit alone
And scoop up food with a spoon;
Don't talk while you eat.
Sit up straight,
Keep hands on lap and
ELBOWS OFF THE TABLE

E e

If someone's stuff is missing,
Owning it, is stealing it.
Be a cheerful giver;
Finders can't Be Keepers.

Take a break and take a nap;
Sleeping is refreshing.
30 minutes is good for napping,

GO TO BED WITHOUT FUSSING

Play "catch" with a ball,
But don't throw rocks or toys.
Throwing things might get friends hurt;
Always HAND STUFF OVER

Hh

It is rude to cut in
While someone else is speaking.
Here's a really good advice,
Interrupting Is Not Nice

A laugh is a blast
For pranks and gags;
Chuckles are good for bloopers,
But...

Jokes Should Never Hurt Others

When a door is tightly closed,
Even when it's slightly closed;
KNOCK AND WAIT TO HEAR,
"COME IN"
Then open the door.

Be attentive, don't be antsy.

LISTEN CLOSELY

To hear what the speaker say.

Don't insist or resist;
Say it once and wait.
"MAY I?"
IS A GOOD WAY TO ASK.

Mm

A rule for men and boys;
Gentlemen, big and small,
No Hats At The Table, Please.
It's poor manners
To wear a hat while eating.

Nn

Rules are Dos and Don'ts to follow;
When at home, at play and at school.
Follow the clues; Obey Rules.

O O

Stop.
Look.
Listen.
Pay Attention
Every Time.

P p

QUIT WANTING TO BE FIRST

All the time, every time.
Let others try their best,
Don't take too long a term.

Qq

Do not bully, do not cheat;
Do your best when you compete.
Do not spit, push or hit;
Role-model kindness To Others

Rr

Share Your Toys

And play as a team.
If you win and others lose,
bragging isn't courteous.
Be a team player.

"Thank You" and "Please"
Are Good Courtesies
Then when someone thank you,
Say, "You are welcome."

T t

You must not cuss or tease or fuss,
Or call others names they won't like.
Be sure to give a compliment;
Use Positive Words

**Families do things their special way;
Be it religion, culture, or race.**

Views of Others
Must be handled tenderly.

It's always good to respect and embrace.

Just don't help yourself alone,
Look out for playmates too.
And try not to jump ahead,
Calmly, wait your turn.

When you burp or if you fart,
Or someone's in your way;
When you want to join a conversation,
Or want someone's attention;
"eXcuse me,"
is a key phrase.

Answer nicely
When you are called,
"Yes"
sounds better than
"yep" or "yeah"

Y y

Playtime is fun time,
Climbing like a chimp;
Pretending you're a carousel,
Moving round and round.
Jump! Run! Roll like a drum!
Active games are played outside,
Zoom! Zoom! is for outdoors.

Zz

One-liners
Are Easy To Memorize

A Arrive On Time

B Be patient

C Close Doors Quietly

D Don't Pout

E Elbows off the Table

F Finders Can't Be Keepers

G Go To Bed Without Fussing

H Hand Stuff Over

I Interrupting Is Not Nice

J Jokes Should Never Hurt Others

K Knock And Wait For A, "Come In."

L Listen Closely

M "May I?" Is A Good Way To Ask

N No Hats At The Table, Please

O Obey Rules

P Pay Attention

Q Quit Wanting To Be First

R Role-model Kindness To Others

S Share Your Toys

T "Thank You" and "Please" are Good Courtesies

U Use Positive Words

V Views of Others Must Be Handled Tenderly

W Wait Your Turn

X "eXcuse me," is a key phrase

Y "Yes" sounds better than "Yep" or Yeah"

Z Zoom! Zoom! is for outdoors

Congratulations!
You've learned all your
GOOD MANNER ALPHABETS!

Here's your certificate,
You are a Super Polite Kid!

Join Team-Sapo

email Sapo
kid_sapo@yahoo.com

email Ms. Lewis
ophie2020@yahoo.com

Meet the Author

Photo by Portia Langley

Ophelia S. Lewis is a poet, essayist, and creative writer who writes for both grown~up audiences and children. Besides writing, she loves to read, watch sports, play video games and cross-stitch. Most of her cross-stitch needlepoint of interesting subjects are auctioned to fund the different humanitarian projects she's involved with—Better Day Academy school building project in Liberia, West Africa (www.betterdayacademy.wordpress.com), Sapo Books-for-Kids Campaign, and PJ's and Blanket Project in Brooklyn Center, MN (www.pjsandblanketproject.org).

GMA is Ms. Lewis' second children's book, but she's working on more; including Korlu Learns to Fly, and her newest series, Adventures at Camp Pootie-Cho. Please visit her website(www.ophelialewis.com) for updates. Ms. Lewis lives with her family in Georgia.

Printed in Great Britain
by Amazon